I0838986

# Safe Sex Saves Satan

By

## Larry A. Yff

# CHAPTERS

# INTRODUCTION

3

The goals of this book are to put you up on game.  The *game* is sex, and to be honest...it's not a fucking game at all.  If you follow the rules you live.  If you don't follow the rules you die.  If you cheat you die.  If you make your own rules you die.  This book will show you how to follow the House rules for sex so you can have a constructive home life, enjoyable social life and successful career.  Yup...it's all related to good sex...not safe sex.

<u>**CHAPTER ONE**</u>

**God is the House**

The term "house" is used to refer to "the person who makes the rules."  If you've ever been to a casino, the "house" is the casino.  The House lets the players know what the games are and the rules of the game.  Typically, the House sets the game up in a way so that in the long run it always wins.

In my view, God is like the House.  Now, in order for this to make any sense, you have to know one thing and not know another.  The one thing you need to know is that humans did NOT create this Earth.  That's simple enough.  The thing you don't have to know is how to gamble.  I say that because I use a lot of gambling terms and situations in this book.  It seems fitting because a lot of people live their life like it's a game of chance.  A gamble.

Once I decided to take the view that God created everything, I began to view Him as being the House.  When you create something, you know what's best for it.  You know exactly how it should be used so that it does what you say it will do.  Your name and reputation are on the line if you are the creator.

So if I'm saying God created the Earth and everything we see and don't see, I am in essence saying God is the House.  He is the one that knows how everything works.  He is the one who knows every procedure, every practical use for every square inch of this planet because I believe He made it.  He sets the rules.

With the casino as the House, the rules are designed for you to lose.  The main goal of the casino is to make money.  The casino does not give a shit if you were on a hot streak and then fell the fuck off and lost your favorite daughter's school clothes money.  All the house wants to do is to get your cash.

When you play at a casino, there are certain rules you have to follow; while there are other rules you have free will as to how you want to play.  Of course the House suggests that you play the rules the way they designed the game to be played.  They go so far as to have YouTube tutorials on "how to play blackjack correctly and win" or "how to" classes on the proper way to shoot dice so you can be a winner the majority of the time.

The bottom line is that the House sets the rules for its advantage and for a desired result.  Remember when I said I view God as being the House?  Since I see Him in this view as it regards to Earth, I am saying He has rules for how everything related to the Earth should function.  When things don't function the way they are supposed to, it will make Him look very bad.  It will make Him, a Being we already have never seen, and the Creation Story in the Bible seem like a fairy-tale book and make Him out to be some sort of fictional character.

Have you ever noticed that every time something good happens, people have a tendency to 1) thank God or 2) view it as being the norm?  This is because we all have a sense that the Earth and the Universe has some type of order to it.  We all sense that everything on Earth, including us humans, has a purpose in the grand scheme of things.  What we don't all agree on is who the House is.  Even when we don't say out loud who the House is, we subconsciously believe there is a House.

House rules are evident everywhere you look.  There is a type of natural calm when we see the House rules at work.  When we see a bird flying, we don't tend to get super excited.  It's expected.  They were designed with wings and therefore we expect them to fly.  That is the norm.  That is the House rule for birds:  fly.

It's when we see something unnatural that we begin to react.  For instance, when we see fish or squirrels "fly" we tend to lose our shit.  "I promise on my mama...that fish literally flew out the water!  I know what the fuck it sounds like but that fish

actually had wings!  I'm a grown ass man.  I don't have to lie to

you!"  Those tend to be the conversations when you see

something that appears to go against logical House rules in

nature.  Those instances are called a freak of nature or the better

term is simply unnatural.

There are actually fish that *appear* to fly because they do

shoot out of the water super high and do have fins that look like

wings and those wings actually flap a little...but they aren't *really*

flying.  There are also squirrels that have large flaps of skin

between their front and back feet and when they jump from a

tree and do their free-fall thing, they use those flaps like wings

and actually do kinda fly from one tree to the next...but they

aren't *really* flying.  That activity is restricted to birds because they

were designed by the House with wings to fly, and when they are

doing what they were designed to do it's a beautiful thing.

That's the beauty of being the House.  You set the rules and you do so for a desired result.  Taking the bird example a step further, since birds are designed to use their wings to fly, they tend to be in high places and, as some would say coincidence would have it, there are things called trees on Earth.  These trees are large plants that reach up to the sky and are the perfect place for birds to make their homes.  Birds love that shit!  They fly around and look for high places to call home.  It could be a tall ass tree or a big ass hole you have in your roof that they choose to make their home.  When a bird does make its nest in your hole in the roof, you can't even get mad.  It's what you expect:  birds fly high and live in high places.  All you can do is call your local roofing company and get your shit fixed.

The House.  God made trees and birds and they are both perfectly designed to work together.  Those House rules God has in place are called natural.  There are rules in nature that, when followed naturally, make us not even look or think twice about it.

On the flipside, if we see a House rule in nature not working, like in the *flying* squirrel and fish example, we tend to view it as a freak of nature.

Trees aren't just birdhouses.  They play an essential role in all life.  Trees process the air, cleaning it of bad chemicals through a process called photosynthesis.  Without this process, the air would be more full of toxins, so much so that humans wouldn't be able to breathe it.  Trees also prevent erosion.  Their roots keep the ground below them stable.  There are also a lot of everyday products we get from trees:  lumber for building, molasses, fruits like apples and paper products.  It's hard to imagine life without toilet paper, but that's how we would be living if it weren't for those big ass plants we call trees.  They *definitely* were designed to have a purpose here on Earth.

There's something about watching natural House rules in action that relax and amaze me.  The purpose and design of House rules in nature directly reflect the intentions of the designer.  Remember, the House sets the rules for a reason.

When you see how all the House rules work in nature without any

type of verbal communication it's a beautiful thing.  It becomes

apparent that the House rules for nature are not evil or

destructive in nature.  They are designed to all work together to

maintain and sustain this thing we call life.  It makes you marvel at

how infinitely intelligent the House must be.  Since I believe the

House is God, it makes me respect and admire God's ability and

helps me stay the course in life knowing God designed me for a

purpose, and if His design for me is a portion of the design He has

in nature...my life is gonna be one for the record books!

I love to watch documentaries about big cats like lions and

tigers.  There are a couple of things about big cat life that stand

out to me.  One is when male lions kick the young male cubs out

of the family territory and the other is when male lions kill the

young cubs of the new female lions they want to mate with.

When a male lion cub reaches a certain age where he's thinking about having sex, the pride (that's what a lion family is called) males/fathers kick the sons out.  This process is essential to prevent in-breeding, controls family size and creates solid family structures.  The sons are now forced to find their own food and hopefully team up with other outcast young male cubs to form coalitions.  That gives the young males the best chance to survive.  This process is also important because it is the testing period for young males.  The males who survive this period are rough, confident and know how to fight and kill.  These are all important traits a pride male must have to keep his family safe and to protect his territory.

The other thing about lions, and male lions in particular, is when they do this thing where they go from royal King of the Jungle to baby-killers.  When a group of male lions band together, they do so for protection and to have sex.  Not sex with each other:  they want to combine their strength to take over a territory so they can mate with the female lions (lionesses) that stay there year-round.  (Quick side note:  females pretty much stay in the territory they were born in.  They eventually mate with the new males who have violently taken control over the females land.)  When male lions take over new territory, they instinctively know they must first subdue the females, then kick out any adolescent-age males or kill them and then they must undertake the bloody task of killing all cubs, male or female, under the age of about a year old.

When the cubs are killed, it triggers something in the female lions.  Something in their design makes the lady lions want to mate with the new males and have the new male's cubs.  That is exactly what the new males are hoping to achieve.  Once again, this is an essential step for the new males because their goal is not to raise anyone else's cubs, but to pass on their own genetic code that nobody directly told them how to do and why.  It just comes programmed into being a male lion by design.  It is proven that biologically females are able to mate with the new males and not allow their eggs to get pregnant until the new males have proven themselves to become good providers and protectors. This also seems to be programmed into the brains of female lions by design.

My question is, "Who taught the lions how to do this?" Lions don't talk to each other or have sex education or good parenting classes, so how are they able to know when to start these processes and what's the importance of them?  When I see these things naturally, it always makes me think about design. There *has* to be some sort of design in nature.  And if there is design in nature, there must also be a designer.

Once again, you have to look at the results of the House rules.  Do the rules create chaos or do they have a good purpose? Looking at the results of House rules will let you know the heart, intelligence and motivation of the House.  Even in the example of cub-killing, you can see the basic need for that process and that it's not just designed to kill cubs just to be killing them.

I could go on for a thousand pages about the beauty, creativity, intelligence and functionality of God's House rules in nature…but I won't.  The list would go on forever.  I *could* talk about how God created a light so we can function in the daytime called the Sun and a night-light of sorts called the Moon so there is a little bit of light for night-time activities.  I *could* talk about how if the Earth was just a little closer to the Sun we would all burn to death or if we were a little farther away from the Sun we would all freeze to death as a point of proof of a designer.  Or I could even talk about how essential the laws of gravity, rainfall, the periodical elements and other aspects of nature clearly show there is a design and a designer…but I won't.  Just know that if you don't get the message that everything about life has a design and purpose, you are denying and limiting the value of your life.

It is clear that the House rules are meant for good.  It is clear that the House is operating on an intelligence level no human or artificial intelligence can mirror or comprehend.  It is also clear that the House rules were set in place to support life.  It is also clear that if you are reading this book you fit into the classification of life and therefore, you were designed for a specific purpose and the sooner you get in tune with the designer, the sooner you can do what you were truly designed to do.

## CHAPTER TWO

### Satan is the Card Counter

Satan is *definitely* the card-counting schemer in the casino example. Why he fits the bill is what needs to be looked at and here's where it can get tricky. Many people don't believe in God or Satan but somehow still believe in things they can't see, have never seen or are make-believe. I personally believe in the presence of God, Jesus, the Holy Spirit, angels, demons and Satan like most people believe in Santa Claus, the Easter Bunny, the Tooth Fairy, Hercules or Bigfoot.

If you have a basic knowledge or belief of the Bible and God, this section will be fairly easy for you to follow and glean some hopefully pretty helpful information from. If you are more of a believer in Santa and not so much God, angels or Satan...I think the basic concept of what I am showing you will make enough sense for you to begin to dig a little deeper if you are feeling lost and looking for any possible solution to helping you find your purpose and be successful in life.

The Bible tells us how Satan got mad at God and wanted to experience worship and power like God does.  He began to get jealous and started to turn angels away from worshipping God to following him.  What follows is my version and I'm not claiming it is 100% Bible-based.  As you know, God found out and was like, in the words of Denzel in the movie Training Day when he was letting everybody know that he runs shit, "King Kong ain't got shit on me!!"  After God made some statement like that He proceeded to kick Satan's ass out of Heaven and *that* is how Satan came to Earth and he's been on the warpath ever since.

You may not understand or believe in the Satan's Fall event, but just imagine this scenario:  You are at work and you believe you can run the company better than your boss.  In fact, you know you can because you've watched him for a couple years now and you can see all his faults.  You're so confident, you get a bunch of fellow employees to agree with your dumb ass.  The boss finds out and fires you and everybody who listened to you.  What's at stake?  Your pride, reputation and your name.  Here you are jobless and now the people who followed you are mad too.  Since you were prideful at your old job, you will most likely be prideful still and do whatever you can to 1) personally show your old boss that you are his equal and can run a company better than he can, and 2) show your followers that you deserve to be followed, worshipped and respected because of your leadership skills and ability.  That's where we pick the story back up about Satan:  his mission is built on being prideful, vengeful, publicly embarrassed and resentful and now he wants as many people as possible to link up with him and give him respect...or at least *not* link up with God and give God respect.

Circling back to the casino reference, a Card Counter is a person who studies cards, has a good memory, is good with data retention and, no, fuck all that...a Card Counter is a cheat plain and simple.  His goal is to find ways to go around the casino house rules so he can make money.  Card Counter's focus on the poker game of blackjack.  This is a card game where, depending on how many card decks are being used, you can potentially keep track of what cards have and have not been played.  Knowing this shapes your play.  If you "know" there are a lot of high cards left in the deck, you will not take a hit on your hand because the chances of you losing will be higher.

Have you ever heard the saying, "cheaters never prosper"?  It's true.  You may win for a little while, but in the end it's not worth it.  First off, your motivation is thrown off.  All you're interested in is beating the system somehow.  If it's gambling, you want to try and beat the system to win money.  If it's cheating on a test, you're trying to get a passing grade when you don't really deserve it.  Card counting works to a certain degree.  In fact, if you count cards correctly, your chances of winning goes up so slightly that it's really not worth it.  If your chances of winning any given blackjack hand is 51%, if you count cards your chances may improve to winning 53% of the time.  People who are greedy look to capitalize on that very small window and risk all the money they brought to the casino just to win an extra 2% of the time.  If you're playing with hundreds of thousands or millions of dollars, that small percentage *can* add up.  On the flipside, card counting is not an exact science and you could just as easily fuck off your rent money and life savings no matter how well you count cards.

Here's where we tie this in to Satan.  Remember he is the disgruntled employee in the scenario we talked about three paragraphs earlier.  Feel free to circle back to refresh your memory.  Alright, Satan is disgraced, disgruntled and embarrassed and wants to get back at God.  His mission every single mutha-fuckin'day is to keep you from giving God respect.  Satan doesn't need you to give him respect.  In fact, he kinda likes it better when you don't believe in him; because if you don't believe he exists, then you most likely won't believe in God and that means he can lead you off track and away from your purpose and you'll be clueless as to how to get your shit back that God had planned for you.

He now is trying to find anything he can to increase his odds of getting you away from God and if he can get you to directly worship him over God, well, that's just the icing on the cake.  There are stories in the Bible where, wait a minute.  Before I go further I think it is very important that I explain to the average person what the Bible really is.

People think the Bible is a religious book that God wrote through His followers thousands of years ago.  You would be right and wrong.  The Bible is actually more like a book series.  There were thousands of religious/spiritual books written, studied and passed down for thousands of years regarding the beginnings of humanity, who God is and how He interacted with humans.  It would be unreasonable to publish a book called the Bible that contains thousands of manuscripts, so the consensus was to narrow it down to the manuscripts that were 1) written by eyewitnesses, firsthand accounts to the life and times of Jesus, 2) could be proven historically, 3) gave the reader an overall understanding of God, creation and Jesus and 4) was limited to around 60 books.  THAT collection of books is what the Bible is made of.  There are about 30 different authors of the manuscripts who lived in different time periods and lived in different parts of the world.  All of the information in the Bible is from them, their collective stories jive together and even though they span all these timeframes and countries, they have all been proven to be historically accurate.

Getting back to the Card Counter.  The Bible tells us stories of where Satan tries to do whatever it takes to try and gain just the slightest "advantage" over God.  He never actually gets the advantage; but what he is successful at is making sure God doesn't get the credit, glory, honor and respect He deserves.

These tactics range from asking God for permission to harm certain people and/or take away their wealth and kill their families just to see if they will stop honoring God or not.  That specific story can be found in the Bible in the book of Job.  I know some of you may not believe the Bible is the best source to prove God's glory or Satan's scandalous activities, so let's switch gears and focus on today's world.  By today's world, I'm referring to the time period from about 1900 to 2021 because this book is written in 2021.

For these examples, you don't have to necessarily believe in God, Jesus, the Bible or Satan...all you need to do is need to see if the scenarios make sense.  When I went through this process, it allowed me to understand what was going on behind the scenes in the news, politics and the business world clearer.  This clarity allowed me to not get distracted from recovering my purpose and destiny from the shit-show that is called my past.

Let's look at the media.  If you watch the news, you will think the whole world is full of rapists, murderers, cheaters and corruption.  You tend to get the idea that the world is going to shit.  The majority of news shows start off with "eye-catching" news first.  This tends to be the stories of whose mom was murdered in cold blood by her children, or who cut the head off a baby and ground the baby's body into hamburger patties and stored them in the freezer in the basement.  The last two minutes the news is lighter.  Typically we hear about somebody who saved a beached dolphin from dying or about a dog who starts to dance every time he hears Eminem.

We talked about objectives earlier.  What is the media's objective in telling us about all this chaos and mayhem?  And the bad news is these channels are streaming this bullshit live every mutha-fuckin' hour of every mutha-fuckin' day twenty-four hours a day every mutha-fuckin' year!  It used to get exhausting and discouraging as fuck UNTIL.  It wasn't until I began to believe the

Earth has a designer and that designer is God.  Then I began to dissect the House rules God put in place and believed the objective of those rules were for the good of society and nature.  Then I began to look deeper into why are we being bombarded daily with stories of murder and violence like it's the norm?  And that is also when I began to believe that there is some type of evil and deceptive force at work on Earth.  Since I had already concluded it was not God, Jesus, the Holy Spirit or angels, I had to look at who it could be.  Since I deeply believe in God and other entities that operate outside our physical realm as being real, the reality that Satan and his band of misfit demons exist makes sense and follows that same line of reasoning.

The Satan's Fall story in the Bible laid out Satan's motivation and also provided many eyewitness and historically proven events where evil-doers were hard at work trying to wreak havoc on the Earth, our purpose for being here and on any type of spiritual belief we may or may not have established.  The media seems to be the area where I began to see the most corruption, with Big Business a very close second and the Church right behind that; kinda making it a 3-way tie for the "Top 3 areas Satan uses his Influence" award.

To be clear when I say media, I am also referring to movies and television and not just the news.  Their objectives are clear, corrupt, misleading, dismal and have nothing positive in them *except for*:  making money and influencing all the major areas in society.  I said those last two objectives are positive because making money and influencing society in themselves is not a bad thing.  The Bible teaches us how to create wealth and how to influence society, making those objectives by nature good and honorable goals if carried out with a moral compass.  It's when those two objectives are used to try and discredit what God has done is when they become destructive, unnecessary and evil in nature.

Since this book is designed to talk about how Satan is hyper-focused on using sex as his go-to for causing chaos on the Earth and to try and discredit God's design, we need to take a quick look at how this works in the media, Big Business and the Church.  We will double-back and hit these three main areas a little more in the last chapter where we contrast God's House rules with the activities Satan tries and uses to gain an unattainable leg up on God.

The media.  The media's goals are very apparent like I said earlier.  Their objectives appear to obvious so as to make it seem like it's human nature with nothing spiritual or intentionally deceptive behind it.  The media does this by programming us to expect to see murders and rapings every day at the top of the hour simply because it's human nature and all we, the media are doing is showing people what the world is becoming.  Like they say, "We don't make the news, we just show it and make billions of dollars from it."  What if...what if there was something more sinister at work behind the constant flooding of bad news to our brains every minute of every day?  What if...what if a being named Satan actually did exist and that he is trying to do everything he can to make us think the world and humanity aren't worth shit and that we're just a bunch of degenerates, child molesters and do anything for a dollar?  What if...what if he sees that it's working?

Let's touch on the subject of sex and the media.  We will go deeper into the possible motivations behind "sex sells" strategy on the media, but for now let me give you an example or two.  There was a commercial for a type of floor mop.  The colors of the packaging and the mop were blue and green I think.  They had a cute, basic-looking female with a nice ass in some tight blue jeans and a green shirt who was dancing around the house while she was mopping the floors.

Now, my wife likes to keep a clean house but I have NEVER seen her that excited about doing housework like that.  To be honest, it made me want to buy her that mop just to see if *maybe*

she would want to put on a pair of her sexxxy jeans and start

dancing around the house and shaking her ass while she sweeps

the floor.  My point is, there are the simplest of commercials that

tie sex into their product and it's not by accident.  Companies

spend millions of dollars doing research just to see what kind of

females or subliminal sex messages will affect their target

audience to make them want to buy their product.  It's

unscrupulous and downright perverse at times.

There is a new phenomenon hitting the television world

called "reality tv".  It began when a bunch of script-writers either

got fired or went on strike.  Hollywood and the media didn't want

to stop the flow of cash and came up with a name for television

that was *real,* had no script so as to appear natural and if fake as

shit.  I won't go on about how mindless and fake it is during this

section.  These shows made the list because of sex.

Every commercial, and every episode I've glanced at, highlighted a bunch of women who are constantly showing off their new, fake titties, asses and lips for the camera.  The conversations always seem to circle back around to sex, or who has the best ass-job or who needs to get a tittie job.  I actually was *watching* an episode with my wife and one of these women was bragging about how she used to be a stripper and how she got some work done on her clit.  Every time somebody got mad at her, they would say a snotty remark to her that had something to do with her fake clit.  And since I am all about honesty, I have to say, I have gotten caught up watching it because it's on the television in the bedroom and it's kind of like an addiction:  I keep watching and saying to myself, "maybe this episode will actually contain some real conversations that aren't scripted for the camera.  Being a married man, the big assess and titties don't excite me on any sort of lust level, *but,* it does make the show a little more palatable.

I may have mentioned this before, but it stands out so much, I will mention it again.  How many times have you watched a commercial for a sports bar that has a bunch of hot-ass waitresses serving plates full of spicy Buffalo wings and alcohol to some average-joes who came to watch the game.  The message is: if you want to see hot chicks who love sports and love to serve your drunk ass beer on game night, come to our sports bar and spend your money with us.  We are the sexxxy ones.  We have the sexxxy women.  We have plenty of beer for you to get drunk on.  It's better watching the game at our bar because of all these factors.  My purpose for mentioning sports bar examples are because you don't get the message that it's just a nice place to be…what makes it a good place to be and good times is the sexxx appeal and the alcohol.

I already have my view on the media and I'm not here to push my view on you.  I am simply opening you up to a new way of thinking that may or may not change your life.  I don't watch the news at all.  I hear about the chaos from friends or if I am

watching a show, I will be forced to see some of the bullshit lies

and chaos the media and Satan are trying to push on me and I

usually mute my television until the commercials are over.  All I

know is that when I changed my view on God, the media and

Satan was the turning point for me where I began to see the

beauty in God's design of the Universe and was able to have

encouragement that I could live out God's plan for me.

That's my view on the media and Satan.  Now let's touch

on Big Business for a hot second.  It's no secret about the

corruption in Big Business.  It's as though, once again, we are

being programmed to assume it's the norm and that people

running Big Business are just doing what human nature does best

and that is make as much money as possible with as little regard

to morality as possible.  We are being trained to accept the

influence Big Business wields in our everyday lives.  It's as though

we are being groomed to take it up the tailpipe with no grease when it comes to the evilness Big Business inflicts on us on an

everyday level.

I don't' want you to think I am hating on Big Business and

that it's all from the devil.  I LOVE Big Business.  In fact, God has

given my wife and me some Big Business plans that are designed

to restructure every aspect of how Big Business is done until it

goes along with God's original design for it.  We are going to do

real estate development, change the entire agricultural farming

world on its' head and clean out governing agencies that aren't

doing their jobs of protecting consumers from predatory

producers and lenders.  Without business, capital and commerce,

the world systems would not operate.  Business is essential; but

what's not essential is the level of deceit and disregard for human

value.

Big Business routinely pays agencies like the FDA and

USDA, agencies designed to protect America's consumers, to

allow products on the market that are harmful to consumers just so they can make money.  If the FDA is supposed to only allow

good food and drug products on the market, can somebody

please explain to me how in the good fuck can a pill that treats (it

doesn't cure at all…) one disease have 18 negative side effects

and cause other diseases?

We all see the commercials for these drugs that the FDA,

the media and Big Business allow to flood our markets but feel

hopeless to stop them even when we know they are horrible.  It's

as though we just succumb to the power and influence of Big

Business and continue to take it up the ass.  I saw one for ED.  For

those of you unaware of what ED is let me simplify it for you:

your dick doesn't get hard because of poor blood-flow or stress.

The pill said it will help you get your dick hard so you can

start having sex again BUT you may get a rash, an oily substance in

your bowels, your piss may contain blood, shortness of breath,

temporary blindness, migraines, short-term memory loss, blood-

clotting that may result in death…but at least your dick can get hard again and that's what's important.  Once again, I'm not here

to put the blame on Satan BUT I am here to tell you to just try and

think outside the box a little more.  What if...what if the goal of

Big Business in the legal drug industry was to keep our bodies full

of harmful drugs so that we can't focus on our purpose in life?

What if...what if there was some type of force operating behind

the scenes of Big Business that just doesn't give a fuck about you

or what you do and only wants to get you hooked on drugs as

your only solution to certain situations and away from God's

natural solutions He designed for you?  What if...what if Big

Business was being used just for the sole purpose of making

humanity think that Big Business is some type of entity that we

can't control or stop so we might as well keep our pants down to

our ankles and a jar of Vaseline nearby?

I'm not here to say Big Business is from Satan.  I'm just

saying "what if?"  Big Business is only a collection of humans

banding together to conduct an agenda.  What rules for operation those humans follow determine the positive or negative effect Big Business will have in society.  What if…what if we humans began to band together and form businesses that had God's agenda as our agenda?  What would Big Business look like?  What products would be allowed on the market?  If that new agenda based on God's House rules are anything like the rest of God's House rules…Big Business could possibly become the most important tool on the planet to improve the standard of living for all humans in a competitive and equal market.  What if…

The church made my list as an area where Satan uses deception and sex education his tools to spread his influence. When Jesus talked about "building up His church" and that "He loves His church like a groom loves his bride", He was referring to a church that is the exact opposite of what we call church today. The term church Jesus mentioned referred to a "body of citizens who had influence."  These citizens were like a council who all had voting power and used it to influence society.  The church today has no influence what so fucking ever in society when it comes to legislation, and particularly legislation that deals with sex.

The pastor is the leader of the church and he is supposed to teach the church body how to use its influence to take over new territory for God.  The Lord's Prayer says, "...may Your Kingdom come and may your will be done on Earth like it is in Heaven..."  Jesus told us to pray that prayer daily.  In essence, He was teaching us that we need to daily ask God to use us to 1) establish a physical version of the Kingdom of Heaven here on Earth and 2) enforce God's will through the Kingdom of God. (Quick side note:  the Kingdom of Heaven is a place; while the Kingdom of God refers to God's influence.)

Taking that a little farther, Jesus came here to take care of legal business.  This is very apparent in His first sermon.  His first sermon served as sort of a Mission Statement that a business would use or kind of like a speech a President would make when he takes office.  His opening line and closing line both referred to the Kingdom of Heaven.  Later on in His career when He sent 72 of

His disciples on a mission, He told them, "...when you go into a

town and heal people, tell them the Kingdom of God is near".

He's telling them to tell people, and show them by their actions,

that God's influence is here and it is God's influence that has

given us the power to do miracles.

Here's how the church ties into my whole message about

sex.  It is the church's responsibility to uphold the laws of God in

the Bible.  It is the church's responsibility to teach the

congregation how to influence society with God's laws.  When an

issue arises that goes against God's laws, the church is supposed

to use its' influence and shut down any attempts to change or

pervert God's laws.

I live in Michigan.  When there was a bunch of talk about

legalizing homosexual marriages, I never heard the church say

anything in protest.  When it was time to vote on legislation

regarding homosexual marriages, the church sat there quiet as a church mouse.  The church didn't exercise any influence in thwarting attempts to turn marriage, which by God's definition and design is reserved for a man and a woman, into an institution for two dudes, two females or any other combination of persons society deemed as having access to marriage.  What I did see was Hollywood flexing its' muscle and pushing hard as fuck for the legalization of homosexual marriages and they did an excellent job of it.  The way Hollywood used its' money and media power to support homosexual marriage and influence homosexual marriage legislation is the same way the church was supposed to stand up *against* the legalization of homosexual marriage.

That wasn't even a battle.  It was more like a teenage schoolyard bully taking a 1st-grader's lunch money.  Instead of the church body taking a stand, Church's Chicken might as well have stepped in and represented the entire church body.

I won't go too deep into God's rules for sex in this section because we will go into more detail in the last section called "The House Rules for Sex and Love".  What I will say is what

if.  What if...what if there is such a hard push for promoting sex in

the media because somebody has an agenda for it?  What

if...what if Satan, the deceiver, the disgruntled employee really is

on the warpath and wants us to participate in sexual activity that

goes against God's laws because he's still bitter and he knows that

activity is robbing us from carrying out God's plans for our lives?

What if...

# CHAPTER THREE

## We are the Players

God is the House, Satan is the Card Counter and we are the Players.  Many of us think we have no significant purpose here on Earth.  Some of us care while others simply don't give a fuck.  It's easy to fall into the trap of not caring.  I used to not care.

I was raised in a Christian home and prayed before and after each meal, attended Christian schools all the way through high school and went to church as a family twice on Sunday and once during the week on Wednesday nights.  Even with all those sermons being slung my way, when I left the nest and entered the real world, in my view God was not present.  The news was always pumping my eyeballs with messages of sex, scandals or some other type of negative activity.  It was my belief, based on what I saw I movies, other media outlets, the way Big Business was fucking up and what I saw in my everyday life was that God existed 1) just in the church and 2) for the good of white people.

When I was around 20, I was introduced to the Nation of Islam.  It interested me because I was adopted as a baby by white parents.  All my schooling was at 99% white schools with 99% of the staff being white.  My church life was at a church with a 99% white congregation, 100% pictures of white Jesus, God and angels in the artwork and 100% white, male pastors.  Looking for the need to find something black in religion or spirituality that I could take with me and apply it to my life, the Nation of Islam seemed like a good thing.

The Nation of Islam held appeal for me because I know humans have a spiritual side and I also knew spirituality wasn't designed to be racist in any way.  I was finally able to see images of black, male pastors and black people worshipping their god in their own way.  I even began to study history and was able learn that the Garden of Eden was most likely in Africa, the oldest

Biblical writings were found in Africa and the oldest human remains were found in Africa.  This spiritual path gave me pride in my culture and put resentment in my soul against white culture and white Christianity.

After some time though, the whole black versus white thing in spirituality didn't sit well with me and I returned to my Christian roots, but this time I got my lessons and did my gospel-singing with black churches.  Nation of Islam introduced me to what I call black spirituality and that led me to black Christianity.  I loved it!  There were pictures of Black Jesus with black angels in the artwork, the music was more to my style and I got to attend Christian events where there were black families having fun.

The only reason why I went on this spiritual quest was because I am a Player.  I am a Player in the sense that I am on this Earth for a reason and I need to understand what the rules are for me to successfully navigate through this maze, or game, called life.  Every human is a Player *de facto*. Meaning we are Players simply because we are alive and on Earth.  There is design in everything else on this planet so it's just natural that there is a design for humans.

Everyone knows we have some type of spiritual side that goes with our physical side.  We may not all say it's God.  Some of us say it's the Universe or our dead ancestor's guiding us; while others may have a million other rationales and nicknames for the spiritual side of humans.  Regardless, there is an overwhelming consensus that a spiritual calling of any nature is more dignified and worthy of respect than a basic human calling.  For the record, any type of spiritual path, in my view, that uses skin color as a means of hording, monopolizing, distorting or for manipulation still qualifies as a spiritual path:  it's the Players and their moral compass that give a spiritual path its' legitimacy.  We all want to find that path that is proven to give others success, good health, peace, wealth or happiness in life.  Let me simplify.

There were events back in history where Christians went on what they called "crusades".  This is where they looted, robbed and killed thousands of people all "in the name of God."  By putting God into the mix, their thinking was they were doing what was right and noble.  (Interesting fact:  my grade school was Oakdale Christian and we were the Oakdale Crusaders...)  Fast forward to American Slavery and we find white slave owners, white Christian congregations and white Christian politicians justifying slavery because in the Bible we read how, "...slaves obey your masters willing as though you were slaves in nature serving Christ who is your master..."  That ideology back-fired like a mutha-fucka when white Christians began to see and understand the true horrors of slavery in the news; quickly forcing many of them to become Abolitionists and denouncing slavery and the implementation of the Bible into that wicked, American institution.

We tied every other section into gambling and the casino, so this section will be no different.  Players go to the casino to look for something.  They are looking to improve their life.  They are looking for excitement.  They are searching for any opportunity to be able to say they are worthy of a financial blessing and the casino is there to oblige.

The goal for the Player is to bring some money to the gambling shack, freely play games of chance that they know are designed to fleece them of their cash and expect to win.  I know firsthand how this feels.  I loved going to the casino.  I still do actually.  Anyways, I *loved* going to the casino because of the promise of a "free meal".  I'm not talking about the "free meal" you get when you cash in your casino-points to get half off their very full and tasty buffet.  What I'm talking about is the chance, the possibility to just maybe win some money that I didn't have to work for.  I obviously wasn't alone on this.

I would walk in and as I passed people exiting the casino, I could instantly tell who won or lost.  The ones who lost had their hands in their pocket, shoulders slumped forward with their heads down.  A lot of the men had a familiar look because I often had it as I was leaving the casino.  It was that look that said, "Not again!! My baby mama is gonna fuckin' kill me!  Why didn't I stop when I was up!?!  That's it.  I'm not going home.  Maybe I can give myself a black eye and tell my girl I was robbed..."  A whole bunch of dumb ass scenarios would run through my mind on the way home, but it didn't stop me from going back on payday two weeks later to try and see if just maybe 1) the result would be different and 2) once I get up at least $250 I will walk away from the table.

The casino kind of became my church.  It was the place I went to where I could witness a miracle in my life:  taking $500 and against all odds and House rules turning making a profit off it every time I go to the casino.  That was the place where I felt like I had the same chance as anybody else to *make it*.  In my real life, things weren't always going my way and I wasn't getting the breaks I thought I deserved.  I looked to the casino to give me that much needed boost I was looking for.  My Player's search for a boost or a break in life changed once I got out of the church and into the Bible.

Like I like to say:  this is my view and it matters as much as your view does.  I am sharing my view with you based on my experiences in life.  Growing up in the church made it easy for me to get into the Bible.  I already had a basic understanding that there was spiritual activity all around us.  What I hadn't learned in all my years of church attendance was what spiritual acceptance looked like on an everyday basis.  I had been groomed to get my spirituality on Sundays for two hours a day and make sure I prayed before each meal.  Those two things gave me enough qualifications to call myself a Christian.

Earlier I touched on the fact that spirituality, at least in America, had been segregated.  Black Players worshipped in black churches full of black people singing black music with pictures of black Jesus on the walls; while their white counterparts worshipped in white churches full of white people singing white music with pictures of white Jesus on their walls.  Looking at spirituality strictly through a Biblical lens, I saw the beauty and structure in it for all humans.  In fact, Jesus said part of our mission is to, "...teach the Gospel of the good news of the Kingdom of Heaven and make all the nations of the Earth become your students..."

That isn't what any preachers, black or white, seemed to highlight or acknowledge at any church I had ever attended. There was contentment in white churches to deliver a one-hour session full of songs, humor and a sermon that your typical white person could relate to; while the black churches offered the same message appeal to its' black congregation but in a much longer timeframe.  With a white church, you can put your Sunday dinner in the oven, set the oven timer for an hour and when you get home, your family's favorite casserole will be piping hot, ready to serve and eat.  Do NOT try that shit when preparing a meal if you are about to attend a black service.

If you do, please set your timer accordingly.  By that I mean, 1) don't prep the main course of the meal at all before church or 2) set the oven timer somewhere around 3 hours with a main course that is designed to be slow-roasted.  For those of you who aren't pickin' up what I'm puttin' down, let me say it like this: black churches tend to keep going as long as the congregation is still groovin', the drums are still beating, the preacher is still jumpin' around and the spirit is still movin' and shakin' with very little or no regard to time.  You could be in church from breakfast till lunch time.  You could be in church from the hour-long, pre-game, NBA broadcast show until the middle of the 4th quarter.  Put your roast in the oven, set the timer for an hour and take your ass to a black service if you want to.  Your family will be some hungry souls when you return 3 hours later because that roast will be a pile of burnt-ass, crispy-ass, over-cooked-ass meat with black smoke pouring from your oven door.

Getting back to the church…We are Players and we all are searching for the best life has to offer, but when life throws us lemons and we don't have access to water or sugar to make lemonade, well, we tend to devalue this thing called life and devalue anything spiritual with it.  Our rationale becomes, "How can there be anything good out there spiritually when I can't even find anything good physically here on Earth?"  If I can't find success or relief in things I can see, how am I supposed to expect to find happiness in things that I can't see?"

Faith.  Faith is the most productive and useful tool any Player can have if they want to find that right combination of physical and spiritual success in life.  If you believe there is a spiritual side of us that you can't see that needs to work alongside a physical side you can see, you need to have physical and spiritual vision.  Physical vision of course is simple because we all have eyes; while spiritual vision isn't as simple and requires a level of faith.  When I studied the Bible, I began to apply thing called faith to its contents.  I decided to go down the Christian path as a human being, not as a member of any racial or cultural group, and see what I could see.

The first thing I noticed was exquisite, yet simple, structure, planning and design.  The Bible laid out an entirely feasible plan for 1) how human life began, 2) how the Earth was made and who made it, 3) the presence of the spirit realm with individuals from different races and cultures around the world, 4) messages that made sense from someone who had experience in both the physical and spiritual realm and 5) a fairly easy to follow game plan for me to find success in life.  I was able to play the game and respect all Player's from all walks of life and spiritual views.  I still noticed skin color because that's what I see, but I stopped projecting my personal prejudices, biases and expectations on the skin color of other Players and the results were remarkable!

The book of Genesis (and the 1st and 2nd Books of Adam and Eve) documented a lot of God's first interactions with humans.  The laws for living He laid out make perfect sense, and when they followed them, early humanity recorded military victories and personal stories of wealth and success.  When they didn't follow God's laws, the result was a whole lot of losing battles, being taken into captivity and losing both personal and country wealth.  The Bible then goes through other eras in history and details the same processes with people from other cultures.

Fast forward to Jesus time and Jesus gives lessons on creating wealth and a host of other topics that are all based on following God's laws as well.  The unique thing about Jesus teachings is that He actually was in God's presence in Heaven and also lived on Earth.  Most people blow that statement off, but if you take the time to study history from a strictly historical point of view and look at all the evidence of His existence, you will increase that level of faith I was talking about and will be able to find your own spiritual path with your own spiritual eyes.

There was now no hatred toward another cultural group.  I wasn't blaming any other Players for where I was in life.  There was no more wishing I had possessions and successes in life like other Players had because I now knew how to find my own success, with my own God-given skills and that allowed me to appreciate and congratulate others on finding their success.

I began to play the game of life based on the rules God laid out in the Bible.  This wasn't because I had some major revelation where God came into my room as a bright light and talked to me, but because I had read so many eyewitness accounts to the life of Jesus and so many documented and historically accurate interactions between humans and the spirit world that the evidence of God's existence was overwhelming.  I, in my view, would be a fool *not* to take a chance and play life by the set of rules found in the Bible.

This book is focused on God's House rules as they relate to sex and that is where I have to keep my focus.  I could go on forever about how the application of God's rules made so many powerful and positive changes in my life, but the decision to focus on where God's House rules for sexual activity and our success as Players was made because adherence to, or not adhering to, those rules will not only destroy everything positive in your life, but that negativity and chaos will spill over into society and infect the entire world.

# CHAPTER FOUR

## The House Rules for Sex

God has rules for sex and love that can make or break an entire nation.  Some of the first laws He laid out for humans related to sex.  This section will lay out what some of them are and the results of following them or not both in the past and in our modern day.  The crazy thing is that you need rules in order to function.  You can't have one basketball team with 8 players on the court and the other team with 5.  When you drive, you have to follow the rules of the road so people don't crash and burn every 5 minutes.

If the rules are based on equality and are proven to be good, then life is also good.  It's when laws are built on prejudice that fucks up society and breeds hatred, corruption and ignorant activity.  People who have looked at God's rules can see they are meant for good.  The rules aren't meant for you to be miserable; in fact, God constantly says, "...follow My laws so you can have great success and enjoy life..."

People tend to love all of God's rules EXCEPT when the rules relate to sex.  At that point, we tend to just want to do our own thing.  A lot of people don't want to talk about sex and rules because they don't want to offend people; actually, the only area people don't want to touch is when it relates to homosexual activity and that, coincidentally enough, is one of the main areas of sexual activity that are tearing apart the family structure which is the power source and basis of God's plan for Earth.  If you don't like what follows...tough shit.  These are the *Houses* rules for sex.  Not mine.  I just deliver the mail...I don't write it.  And listen, if you're not trying to follow a life according to the Bible, you are free to make your own rules for sex BUT if you want to follow the Bible and you claim to be a follower of Jesus, stop being hard-headed, get your shit together and follow the rules.

House Rule for sex #1:  God created sex to be for a man and a woman, any combination other than that goes against God's design for humanity and is disrespectful.  In the book of Genesis we learn that God told Adam and Eve to, "…fill the Earth with humans…"

How do you naturally fill the Earth with humans?  You have sex.  Sex between a man and a woman naturally create human life and that is the way God designed it to be.  Just to simplify things, men have a dick and two balls with thousands of seeds in them and women have a uterus and a couple dozen eggs in side them.  The man puts his dick inside the woman's vagina and shoots his seed from his balls into her uterus.  After running the gauntlet and surviving a couple of small skirmishes inside the female, the winning sperm, or sperms if you're gonna have twins or more, fertilize the eggs inside the female's uterus and the process of creating a new life begins.  Simple.

What's not simple is two people in a homosexual relationship try and go outside of God's design to create a new life.  Since there is no male in the relationship, the females have to get their sperm from a source outside of their relationship.  Then they have to get that sperm inside whichever female is going to carry it.  Sometimes, the females, in order to have both of their genes passed on, use the female's eggs who aren't carrying the sperm as to imitate that female being the "sperm donor."  Don't quote me on that whole process, but from what I personally have heard and have seen on television, that's the way people involved in homosexual relations have kids as close to naturally as possible.

When something isn't being used the way the designer designed it, the results aren't the same and the process goes against the grain.  When Henry Ford designed the car, he designed it to work with gasoline.  You *could* use diesel because it's what you feel like using...but the car won't operate the way it's supposed to.  I mean, it might still move and function, but not the way it was designed.  Get the picture?

House Rule for sex #2:  Don't have sex with a married person.  This rule also touches on another rule that says, "Marriage is for a man and a woman" because it talks about how a man shouldn't cheat on his wife (a female) and how a wife shouldn't cheat on her husband (a man).

I love God's rules but I broke this one a few times in my day.  The rule makes sense.  It's basic and straightforward.  If someone takes the time to buy a ring, plan a life together and make it legally binding, that means they are serious about each other and want to have a family and grow old together.  This rule rings very true for me because I am now married.  If my wife were to cheat on me after all the planning and shit we've done together...I would destroy a small village to find her and his ass.  We've had this discussion once or twice in a "joking" way and she has let me know the same holds true for her if I were to step outside our marriage; except she added texting is cheating as well…

When you come between that together-forever life-plan it will result in chaos, devastation and possibly murder every time. Let's say a wife is cheating on her husband.  How many times have you seen it on the news and all over the media that the husband gets mad as fuck and kills the wife and/or her lover?  Look at OJ Simpson.  I'm not here to say his wife was or was not cheating, but all the evidence kind of showed she was tip-toeing outside the relationship.  Whether she was justified or if OJ was out fuckin' around is not my call.  All I'm saying is a young man and a wife got killed because a husband felt like his wife was cheating on him.

In the Bible, King Solomon wrote a proverb that said something like, "…young man, stay away from a married woman. If her husband finds out, he will do everything in his power to tear shit up and kill you and/or her.  His rage will burn like a California wildfire…"  It's as though this King, who is recorded in history as being one of the wealthiest and wisest to ever walk the Earth, was

saying the husband is kind of in his legal right to let his emotions

run wild and go into an unstoppable rage if his wife is caught

cheating on him.  If a cheating spouse does get caught and beaten

or killed in a moment of blinding rage, the courts actually allow

the offender to get off with a lighter sentence.

I had to stop having sex with this one married lady

because we felt like the gig was up.  There were subtle signs that

let us know her husband may be on to us.  I love pussy...but not

enough to die for it!  Once again, God's general rules and design

for sex and marriage are for our good health and longevity.

House Rule for sex #3:  Don't have sex with a close relative

like your mom, aunt, sister, nephew of son-in-law.  Once again,

this rule makes sense and is pretty straightforward like the rest of

God's sex rules.  Even if you find your aunt attractive, you have to

admit that having sex with her will cause a shit ton of problems.

In the end, would it be worth it?  What if you got your aunt pregnant?  Now you have to have an abortion OR your uncle now

becomes your father-in-law and the child your aunt has is now

your son instead of being your nephew.  ALSO, if your uncle finds

out he will beat your ass or kill you.

I hope you are starting to see that God's House rules for

sex are good.  You may not agree with them, but if you stop and

look back over your life, you will most likely find the majority of

sex and marriage issues in your personal life and in society stem

from breaking one of these rules.

House Rule for sex #4:  Get married to someone you love

when you are young.  This Rule is not necessarily from God

directly, but it is in recorded by one of the wisest authors in the

Bible who happened to know a lot about sex.  King Solomon is the

one credited with this Rule.  Think about it:  if you get married

when you're young, your sex life and your family life will be

simple.

If you fall in love and have sex and have a baby there's nothing wrong with that.  What if you two breakup and decide to move on?  Both of your lives and the life of that child are not complicated times 10.  If the dad moves on and starts another family, he will have to figure out how much child support he should pay financially to raise his other child in another home and how much time he can spend with that child.  Most times decisions are made through the courts and can get very messy.  Also, how do you think the first child feels?  He or she had mom and dad living in the house each night and now he can only spend time with his dad once or twice a month during a specific time that the courts ordered?

Then there is the issue of sex.  Obviously you are now having sex with a new partner.  This one rings true more for the female.  What if that partner isn't as good or as big "down there" as your first partner?  Now there is the comparison thing going on and it can cause your sex life to have issues.  If King Solomon's rule in the Bible was followed to the letter, the family would stay united and your sex life would be the best ever because there would be nobody else to compare your new partner with sexually.

I could talk about more rules regarding sex and their God-recommended punishment for breaking them but I won't.  My goal is simply to lay out some of God's rules for yourself so you can see if God is being unreasonable and if He created these laws on sex so that you will have a miserable sex life.  The name of this book is "Safe Sex saves Satan" so I will tie all that together in the short summary section for you.

<u>**SUMMARY**</u>

In the beginning of the Bible we learn that God was mad with Satan.  God told Satan that because you deceived Eve in the Garden of Eden that "...her offspring will be your enemy forever and ever.  You will be able to bruise his heel but he will bruise your head..."  Read this next sentence very carefully.  **SINCE GOD TOLD SATAN, "EVERY HUMAN BEING FROM THIS DAY FORWARD THAT WALKS THE EARTH WILL BE YOUR ENEMY", DOESN'T IT MAKE SENSE THAT SATAN WILL WANT TO DO WHATEVER IT TAKES TO ELIMINATE AND KILL HIS ENEMIES EITHER BY KILLING THEM BEFORE THEY ARE BORN OR BE DECEIVING THEM INTO THINKING SATAN, THE TRUE ENEMY OF ALL HUMAN LIFE, DOESN'T EXIST AND THEREFORE ISN'T AN ENEMY AT ALL????**

If Satan can create an environment where humans regularly kill their babies with safe sex options like the Day After pill, abortions or other medical things that are injected either in the bodies of females to prevent pregnancies or in the female uterus to prevent pregnancies, that it would be to his advantage? The more humans are on this planet, the more enemies Satan has to deal with.  There are sooooo many complications females have with these safe sex devices that they should be banned.  Even the "effective" ones that aren't *dangerous* to a female's basic health *still* serve Satan's purpose because the female's monthly cycle is all thrown off or becomes so irregular that the chances of a couple trying to plan and start a family is grossly ineffective and unproductive.

Safe sex options are designed to save Satan because they are focused on preventing life.  Their sole purpose is to allow us an "out" when don't follow God's rules for sex and have to face the consequences.  Safe sex saves Satan by killing all his would be enemies before they get a chance to fight him.  Safe sex saves Satan by molding us to the thinking that God has no major plans or designs for human life and that human life is disposable.

Homosexual activity saves Satan also because 1) females who

could be producing babies (Satan's enemies) don't want to

because that activity doesn't fit the sexual role (the masculine

female) and 2) males involved with homosexual activity aren't

producing new life either because that function does not fit what

they believe their sexual role is.

Abortion.  Abortion is the process of killing a life at an

early stage of development.  "Safe Sex" says this is a good and

safe option because you weren't prepared to have a child, so the

best thing to do is kill it.  There is a place that helps you with this

Safe Sex option structured around abortion called Planned

Parenthood.  Anytime you have an unplanned parenthood, this

place suggests you visit them and make a better plan, a plan to kill

your unborn baby and that somehow qualifies as Planned

Parenting.

God's House Rules for Sex are based on the family and marriage.  How many wives have harmful devices in their uterus or arms to prevent them from having monthly visits from their *friend* or to prevent them to be able to produce new life?  None.  How many married couples have abortions?  None.  When I was single, and even in relationships, I myself was part of several abortions.  Now that I'm married, that is not and never will be an option for my wife and me.  We WANT kids and a family!  We WANT to create more new life that are designed to follow God's plan and to crush the head of Satan's disrespectful ass!  And if you want to be a part of that process and love God the way you say you do, PLEASE stop saving Satan and start following the House rules the way they were designed to make this world a better place by literally creating and establishing the Kingdom of Heaven here on Earth through human life.

**BONUS ESSAYS SECTION:**

# COCAINE & SEX

In the book "Safe Sex Saves Satan", we talked about how our view on sex is important.  We talked about how 'safe sex' can destroy our destiny, but I want to touch on how any kind of sex other than marriage sex the way God designed it will have the same negative effect on our lives.

By now you know I used to do a lot of cocaine.  I smoked crack and sniffed blow.  Doing drugs for me was a double whammy:  I was destroying my health and my sex life.

Some people say I give too many details, but I think it's important to be honest about what the fuck addiction and sex looks like.  It's important because there is a lot of shame around it.  That being said, this Private Matter topic takes off yet another level of shame and guilt surrounding drugs and sex by openly confessing what it is that we do in private.

Every time I got high, I would think about sex.  Those thoughts were saving Satan.  Here's why:  I was living in a dangerous sexual fantasy life and was not interested in using sex the way God designed it.  I know for a fact it wasn't God's design because this is what it looked like:

The second I knew I was about to get some cocaine, my body instantly got a nervous, tingly sensation.  I knew I was about to spend several hours doing something sex-related.  At that point my mind checks out and I get tunnel vision.  At that point for me, it didn't matter if I was supposed to be going to pick up one of my kids from daycare or if I was missing a meeting:  I was about to have a sexual fantasy situation.

So I stop at the spot or have my dope boy come over.  Either way, once I see him, my body would get a relaxed feeling.  There was no more reason to be antsy or anxious wondering if I would be able to hook up with him.  He was here in my face and he only showed up if 1) I had cash in my hand and 2) if he had dope in his pocket.

My first thoughts upon having the drugs placed in my hand was to get one of my favorite porn sites lined up on my phone.  If he had came by to drop off the cocaine, I would barely care what he did from that point on.  He could ask me when should he come back through or some other question, and I would just mumble a response just waiting for him to get the fuck out so I could strip down, do my drugs, watch pornos and play with my junk until the drugs ran out.

There would be an almost possessed mentality once I knew I was alone with my drugs and porn.  A heavy drive to just stare at the porn scenes and take a hit of crack or line of blow and get as much intensity as possible from the rush and transfer that feeling to my dick would be all that mattered.

Once that initial rush would wear down and my heart would slow down, I would instantly get a rush of anticipation and be ready to take another hit or line and stare with a deep intensity on the porn scene again and do the same routine.  I wouldn't be aware of the time or whatever responsibility I was supposed to be doing.  I would remain in my drug/sex trance until...until I noticed I was running out of drugs.

Now I would get anxiety.  ESPECIALLY if I didn't have any more money.  Panic would set in and now my spirit shifted from the intense porn experience to 'how can I get some more money', 'who can I call', 'what excuse can I come up with', 'do I have anything of value my dope boy wants that he can hold until payday or that he can flat out buy?'

Those thoughts would give me a different version of tunnel vision.  I would be consumed with those thoughts until I found a solution or made a phone call that would guarantee me getting more drugs.  While I would wait for someone to send me money or for my dope boy to come back and buy a new coat or piece of jewelry I had for a ridiculously low price or if my dope boy was coming to use my vehicle for a couple hours...I would stare at the porn on my computer or phone screen.

I would stare at it with that possessed intensity again. I would stare at it with an intense excitement. I would stare at it and in my mind I would be telling myself, "...just hold on for a couple more minutes. In a couple more minutes I will be able to feel that sexual rush when I look at one of my favorite scenes." It was an animalistic, non-human intensity that would surround me.

The only thing that would break me out of that grip was when my phone would ring. If it wasn't him, I wouldn't answer. If it was him telling me to come outside in two minutes, I would put my dick back in my pants and be standing by the door, looking up and down the street in anticipation like a dog waiting for his owner to come home.

If he said two minutes and wasn't literally there in two minutes I would panic and call him.  "Hey, I'm standing outside and I if you're gonna be a little longer it's no big deal.  Just let me know and I'll come back outside when you call me back…" just to hear his typical response of, "just relax, I'm at the corner. Stay outside." Click.  He knew he had a product that sold and a customer who would kiss his ass, laugh at his jokes, do some home repair work for cheap or whatever else the fuck he wanted his customer to do because his customer had an addiction and was caught up in it.

He pulls up with the drugs and we're both happy to see each other.  He gets my vehicle and I get my drugs.  Before he pulls off I'm rushing back in the house to get to my pornos.  Pants off, dick out, let's go a couple more rounds.

My phone rings.  It's one of my responsibilities I was supposed to be taking care of.  Now I'm irritated.  I'm irritated because every time she calls it stops my porno!  I switch gears and put a block on my phone for incoming calls.  I am consumed with seeing

more porn and doing more drugs.

Sometimes I would get bold and call a female to do some type

of phone sex thing and would get nervous at the last second and

hide my face from the screen or tell her I would call her later.

Other times I would leave my porn grip and call a female to

confess.  "I have to admit I looked at your cousin, sister, daughter

or friend sexually."  That confession would help me shift gears

sexually.  For the next couple of minutes I would fantasize about

the female from my confession while I did my drugs and watched

my porn...

This process would go on for as long as I had money,

something of value for my dope boy or until I finally just gave up.

I would reach a point where I just felt drained.  Everything was

now moving in slow motion.  I had no more drugs left.  The

excitement and intense sexual thoughts and rush was gone.

Reality would set in and so would depression.

Some of you may have no pity on an addict who now feels

guilty and ashamed for fucking off an entire day or two with no

regards for his or her responsibilities…but I would encourage you

to try.  Try and understand that 99.9% of the time, I believe the

addicted person is physically possessed by some type of demonic

force.

I for one, can guarantee you that I am not myself.  It's more

than just the high.  There is "something" else that keeps pulling

you, calling you, dragging you almost forcing you to stay trapped.

This "thing" keeps you focused on whatever it is you've got

hidden inside of you.

You could have a secret sexual obsession that you can NOT let

anyone know about.  You could have done something in your past

that you are ashamed of and this force combined with drug use somehow is therapeutic.  For every person it's different.  From my experience, the majority of people I would get high with all had something in common:  some type of sex-related trauma, thoughts or experience.

For me, there was the secret sex thing with young females.  Where it came from, I have no idea.  I have never actually had sex with a young female, but the thoughts of it would be there when I was sober and the acts of it would be played out with a super-intensity when I would do cocaine.

That's embarrassing.  That's not a good feeling.  That's a lot of shame and guilt.  That's a feeling of being scum of the Earth.  That's a whole lot of covering up with fake smiles and a focus on flashing money and acting like everything is ok…

The Bible teaches us to "openly confess to one another so we can help each other."  Sex is one of those areas that people do NOT want to confess.  I never confessed any of it at first.  I would just go through the thoughts and acts when I would get high and then I would potentially give a weak-hearted, feeble attempt to reach out and *confess.*  That typically led to more guilt and more craving to get high and keep all those thoughts in my fantasy world.

The reason why I'm sharing this is because God has a destiny for every one of us.

Part of that destiny is to help others.  You can't help others if you are feeling guilty and ashamed.  Guilt and shame makes you feel like you aren't worthy enough to help anyone else while you have all your hidden, bad qualities that you haven't dealt with yet.

Part of that destiny is to create a strong family structure because that is the power base of society.  You can't create that power base if your thoughts and views on sex aren't aligned with God's views for your life.

Me sharing some deep, dark, fucked up experiences is my way of showing others how they can do the same.  I don't suggest you put that shit in a book necessarily; because once you do and it's out there, your ass better be ready to face it all and face it all publicly.  God has given me that level of comfort but I don't think it's for everybody.

Me sharing stuff about sex is also my way of helping people realize the importance your view on sex has for your life.  If you don't get your sex thoughts and views aligned with God's designs, EVERYTHING in your life will be unproductive.  EVERYTHING.  There is no exception.

You can be bad with money and still find success in life.  You can be out of shape and still find success.  You can be old and flabby and still get hot, young chicks to want you.  You can have the *wrong* skin color and still have success.

**Having issues with anything sex-related is the only area where it can and will destroy your finances, your future, your home life, your spiritual life and anything else attached to you having an enjoyable experience here on Earth.  If you stop and really think about it, you will know what I'm saying is true.**

If you are dealing with anything sex-related, PLEASE dig into the Bible and find out how to get from under it.  The Bible is not here to tell you all the bad shit you are doing.  It is a history book that is designed to show you the rules for life from God.  He knows best because He designed it and us.

That is my hope for you as a fellow human that you find peace from sex-related shame and guilt.  I don't care what color you are. I don't care if you're fat as a whale or thin as a rake. I don't care if you have long hair or are bald as a snake.  We are all humans and we all have value.  Thanks for reading this Private Matter.

# ABORTION

Why is there such a big debate about abortion and when human life starts?  This has got to be one of the stupidest debates in the world and that's why I don't get into that discussion.  I may shoot off this Private Matter essay and that's about it.

Let me simplify a couple of key points for you:

1.  **When does human life start?**  Human life starts when a man and a woman have sex and she gets pregnant.  Wasn't that simple?  When a man and woman have sex and she gets pregnant, a human has started its' life.  Oh wait, some of you may have been thinking that a man and a woman can have sex and create a whale?  Or a horse?  Maybe a rhinoceros?  I mean, come on, people.  Debating when a human life starts is a simple question and answer

thing.  We don't need the world's top "thinkers" to help

us in the discussion of when human life starts.  There has

to be more to it than just that...

2.  **Is abortion 1st Degree murder?**  Yes.  Once again, pretty

straight-forward here, people.  If murder is when you

make a plan to kill somebody and you carry it out...that's

1st Degree murder.  Quick question for you:  When you

decided to kill the baby, was it planned out in anyway?

Did you maybe call Planned Parenthood, give them your

information, set up an appointment, got a reminder text

the morning of, came in for the appointment and had the

baby killed?  If so, I'm gonna have to say that's 1st Degree

murder.  Here's another simple example for you:  I get

mad at a guy who stole my girlfriend.  I know the bar

where he likes to have a few drinks.  He likes to get there

at around 6pm and leaves around midnight.  He doesn't

live far from there, so he walks.  I know his exact route.

Just to make sure, I watch him for 3 nights.  On the 4th

night, I casually walk up behind him and quickly let off 2 shots, point-blank in the base of his head with a snub-nose, .38 Special and slowly slip into the car parked near the spot and my friends drives off.  He's dead before he hits the ground.  Everything works as planned.  Is that 1st Degree murder?  If it is, then abortion is murder.

3.  **Is it the woman's right to kill the child?**  Yes.  Since the baby is inside the woman and she's the one who is going to start eating some pretty nasty food combinations, have her nose, feet, knees and ankles get swollen and sore...and let's not forget there will be something living inside her that will be growing, eating and shitting in her...I would *definitely* say she has the choice whether to let the baby human live or kill it.


Since the answers to these questions are extremely simple and straightforward, there has to be something behind the curtain when it deals with abortion.  The key is

to figure out what the fuck it is so we can stop wasting

time with distractions and start using our efforts to enjoy

life and stop killing it.

I'm going to suggest that it's a combination of guilt

and Satan.  I'll do the guilt part 1st because once you

mention Satan, people don't know what to do or say.  Is he

real?  Is he as bad as the Bible says?  Does he really have

the power to influence society?  Getting back to the topic

of guilt…

There is a growing trend in society to baby people.

I'm not talking about little kids, I'm talking about treating

grown-ass people like little kids.

The word "retard" means slow or slower.  If there is a

person whose brain is not developing at the rate it should

to allow him or her to function as an adult, he or she is

classified as being mentally retarded...not a "retard" or "retarded."  See the difference?

One statement is a cold, by-the-book fact talking about a person's trait or characteristic; while the other is a label that takes away from a person's human value and is unacceptable for people to use...*especially* Believers.

How does this relate to abortion?  When you pre-plan and carry out the death of an unborn baby, you are guilty of 1$^{st}$ Degree murder.  That does NOT mean you are a murderer.  It means you are a person who committed the crime of murder.  Yes, you are guilty of that crime; but you are still a person who can 1) take responsibility for the crime of murder, 2) have the guilt aspect of it taken away and 3) you are not a bad, evil person.

People are trying to allow a mother-to-be to kill her child without the guilt.  It doesn't work that way.  Anyone guilty of a crime is guilty.  A crime is a crime and guilt is

guilt.

Let's talk about Satan and abortion.  I will be brief

because if you're interested in this topic more, you can

read the book, "Safe Sex Saves Satan."

I do want to say Satan is a real being and it is proven

that he hates humans.  Why?  Because he is a being who

used to be one of the top-dogs in Heaven and got kicked

out and can NEVER return to that blessed, powerful state

of living.

His only goal now, and he put this on the public record

for everyone to see, is to make sure humans don't get to

enjoy Heaven on Earth or the spiritual realm known as

Heaven.  We are his eternal enemies.

What if...what if he *is* able to influence people?  I mean, what if he was able to influence people to kill their babies?  Wouldn't that help him accomplish his main goal?

Abortion serves Satan *extremely* well:

1. **Abortion kills humans.  Every baby that gets murdered is one less human that can enjoy Heaven...just the way he wants it.**

2. **Abortion creates guilt.  Every woman I know who has killed her growing baby has, on some level, had guilt.  It's a natural reaction to have guilt after killing a baby.  A female can say, "Yeah, girl. I just did what I had to do."  Sounds good, but there's guilt.  Anytime you live with guilt, it makes it hard for you to guide someone else in life.  How can you tell your daughter to have responsible sex...when you had irresponsible sex that led to you killing a baby?**

3. **Abortion is a distraction.  Do you know how much time and resources we waste on this abortion shit?  How about we start focusing on responsible sex???  We do that and there's no more abortion!!**

Yes, I have been involved in abortions.  2 to be exact.

Yes, I have lived with the guilt of it and it makes me hesitant to tell my kids, or anybody for that matter, to have responsible sex...when I've had irresponsible sex that has led to the death of two babies.

Yes, I didn't feel right talking about responsible sex until I got into the Bible and allowed God to help me deal with the guilt of it all.

Oh!  I just thought about something!  Since abortion is 1$^{st}$ degree murder, shouldn't the person be charged with murder?  Why isn't the mother and father charged with murder?  If they are charged with murder, what should the punishment be?  People get prison time for neglecting a

dog or cat...so why shouldn't the parents get prison time?

And if so, how far back can you go to charge somebody

with the crime of abortion?



**That's just something I had on my mind that I**

**wanted to share publicly that a lot of us have talked**

**about in private that needs to be discussed publicly.**

I am married and me and my wife love God and we love sex.  We like to fuck or make love.  We don't like to have sexual intercourse.  Does that mean we don't love God?  Since we made sure we legalized our marriage in a church before God, does using the word "fuck" mean we have disrespected our sexual marriage vows to God?  If we love God, does that mean we are supposed to use King James talk when it comes to bedroom talk?  I don't believe so.

How are Christians supposed to talk when it comes to sex and love?  That is a question that should be debated and discussed in the church.  But the church doesn't know how to talk about it...so I will.

Before I was married I used to tell females, "yes, I want you to suck my dick." I NEVER said, "yes, I would like it if you put my penis in your mouth and receive oral sex from you." I NEVER just pulled my dick out and kind of smiled at her and looked from her mouth to my dick and back to her mouth hoping she would get the idea that I want my dick sucked. I openly said it then and now that I am married, I have to be just as open with her and vice versa.

If my wife just sat there with her legs open waiting for me to suck on her clit without a formal invitation...that shit ain't happenin'. She needs to feel free to express what she wants. I take that back. Actually, when you're married, there is a beautiful code you establish and nothing needs to be said. When I pull my dick out and lay back and smile at her, she knows what to do. When she lays with her legs open and raises her right eyebrow, I know what to do.

Now that I'm married, does that mean I can never say to my wife, "The kids are gone for the night, so you know we 'bout to get our fuck on all over the house.  I want you to walk around naked so I can look at your sexxxy ass all day and when I can't take it anymore, I'm gonna grab you, turn you around, bend you over and fuck the shit out of you."  Is that how married Christians are supposed to talk?  Is that permissible Christian language?

Some of you may think I'm disgusting and that I am not a good Christian because I want to fuck my sexxxxy wife instead of wanting to "have sexual intercourse with my wife."

Some of you may think I'm disgusting and that I am not a good Christian because I want to lick my wife's pussy until she cums instead of wanting to "lick her in her clitoral/vaginal region until she reaches a climax."

Some of you may think I'm disgusting and that I am not a good Christian because I openly tell my wife to "turn around and put your ass in my face so I can kiss it.  I think you have a sexxxy ass and I can't keep my mutha fuckin' lips and tongue off of that sexxxy thang" instead of openly telling my wife "Can you please turn around? I really like your buttocks and I would like it if you would bend over in front of me so I can kiss it.  I just love the sight and feel of your rear end so much that I can't stop kissing all over it."

The point I am trying to make is that I don't believe you have to go all King James in the bedroom when you have sex as a Christian, married couple.  God made sex to be enjoyable.  One of the authors in the Bible said to the men, "get married to the woman you fall in love with as a youth and enjoy her breasts..." Another author in the

Bible said, "the marriage bed is sacred and something for a husband and wife to enjoy however they see fit."

If that's really true, if my wife and I are used to talking a certain love language before we were married, we should feel free to talk in that same language as a married couple if that is the language that makes us comfortable, keeps our sex life strong and keeps us faithful to each other.

If I'm married and have sexual desires that I can't express to my wife, I am going to be inclined to hit the strip clubs and bars more frequently so I can come across a female who "understands" me and who I can enjoy having sex with.  Since marriage is a thing that God supports and created as the power-base of society, we need to be talking about these things BEFORE marriage.

At the same time, there has to be boundaries and limits.  Just because I may want to have anal sex with my wife does not mean she has to comply and take it every week in her ass.  We still have to compromise.  Maybe she takes it like that on Valentine's Day, President's Day and our anniversary or something.  That's for you two to decide.

My point is that it's your marriage and your sex life. The point is, you two need to talk about sex or your marriage will fall the fuck apart.  If you're a guy and secretly want to have sex with other guys, that's some shit your wife needs to know BEFORE you get married.  We should all be at the point where we can share our views on sex and decide whether or not to move on together or get off the train.

Sex is an important element of marriage that needs to be talked about.  When I look back at the people in my church when I was growing up, I can tell you that there

was only one couple, and I won't say who it is, that looked

like they were having sex.  All the rest of the married

couples looked like zombies.  I never saw anybody sneak

and hold hands or saw a couple share a laugh with another

couple and the wife blush and kiss her husband on the

cheek.

I went to an all-white church and that's what I saw.

Anytime I went to white churches, that is the vibe I got.  I

have to go a step further and say I got the same vibe from

all-black churches as well.

My experience with church and sex was that it

never happened until...until somebody got a divorce

because the wife was cheating or the husband had a full-

blown porn addiction that was out of control.  There was a

pastor who committed suicide because he was hooked on

phone sex and spending hundreds of dollars a month.  He

felt guilty and felt like he couldn't share that with anybody.  Kirk Franklin, a famous gospel singer, came out and said he had a major porn addiction.  He had porn videos stashed all around the house behind every television or something crazy like that.  It happens.  It happens to anybody and it needs to be talked about.  It's major incidents like that when you realized people in the church had sex problems or were actually having sex.

I have to add this to be fair, Joel Olsteen has a wife who looks like she wants to have fun sexually, she's attractive and dresses in a modern, conservative-yet-sexxxy style.  That's refreshing to see.  Her husband Joel on the other hand, with his perfectly set and sprayed hair style, bleached white teeth with that permanent smile on his face and that joyful message he delivers every Sunday, looks like he could care less whether they had sex or not.  I mean, they do have a couple of kids as proof, but other than that...you can tell Joe ain't really hittin' that like he's supposed to.

There is a twist to all of this.  When I was in church, it was also the place where I saw plenty of sexxxxy females.  An older friend of mine used to tell me that church was the best place to find a nice female.  I think he must have been talking to a lot of church-going females as well because the single ladies in church had a tendency to dress sexxxy; unlike the married females who tended to want to leave the impression that they were sanctified, highly favored, blessed and content to be married.

It's unreal for us to think a pastor doesn't get turned on by females outside of his wife.  If he didn't, that means he is either into homosexual activity (and should not be in the pulpit) or he is in complete denial of his maleness.

I've asked a couple preachers about this and even though they were married, they still say they see women as being attractive and even sexxxy.  They even admitted to me that they still look at a sexxxy female walking by sometimes.  For them though, they say the difference is their thought process:  just because they are married doesn't mean they don't see recognize female beauty...it just means they understand how serious marriage is and straying from his wife for some sex is not worth falling out of favor with God, destroying a marriage, destroying the power-base of the family structure, causing emotional harm to the kids and a bunch of other chaos that results from lacking sexual discipline.

If you think I'm being unrealistic, feel free to look around your church and see how many couples look like they are having fun sexually.  Look at your pastor and his wife and see if you think he is hittin' it from the back and they are enjoying doing the reverse-cowgirl position or doing 69's.

When I look around congregations, I see plenty of sexxxy women I would like to have sex with (this of course is before I was married).  What I don't see is married couples looking sexually satisfied; especially the pastor. Nine out of ten times the pastor's wife has a dress that drags down to her ankles and a shirt that's long-sleeved and buttoned all the way to the top button…looking like she walked straight off the television show Bonanza, Little House on the Prairie or some other old-school show.

Do I want my pastor's wife wearing short, sexxxy skirts with high heels and a short top so her ass shows? No.  I'm not saying that.  What I am saying is that when a person is having fun sexually, it shows in the way they walk, talk and dress and it would be nice to see a pastor-wife team looking like they are human and like they like sex.

In the end, I think, as one who was sexually irresponsible and a Christian for many years, that it's important that the church grow some balls and takes a stand on sexuality.  Everybody else openly pushes their thoughts and agenda for sex.

People involved with homosexual activity have openly let it be known that they want to teach public school kids at early ages that homosexual activity is cool and it's something that has no negative or confusing impact on the family and society.  Not cool.  Very confusing.

The media has been pushing shows that send us the message that it's okay if you're a man and you feel like a woman...just cut your dick off, get a fake vagina, get some big, fake-ass titties sown onto your chest and BAM!

YOU ARE NOW A LADY!!!  Not.

It's time for somebody to stand up and start talking

about the beauty of waiting to have sex until marriage.

It's time for somebody to stand up and start talking

about how they did have sexual desires that went against

the Bible and God, but they took the time to fight those

feelings and not just fall victim to any and every sexual

desire and urge that came their way.

It's time for somebody to stand up and start talking

about the fact that getting fake titties doesn't make you a

female anymore than getting a fake dick sewn on your

body makes you a man.

Whatever your view is it's important because it's

your view.  We may not all agree, but what we can agree

on is the results.  Start looking at the results of certain

sexual behavior and see if it's a good thing or a bad thing.

Doing this, I believe, will allow the natural design and

order of sex to continue to be a beautiful thing.

It all starts with 1) your view on sex, 2) talking

about sex and 3) making sex education an important topic

in church, the home and schools.

## Superheroes aren't super at all


We love to believe in the power of super humans.  In fact, movies and the media push these superheroes on us as much as they possibly can.  Why?  What if...What if Satan was behind the media?  What would he get out of pushing the belief in Superman and all the other cartoon heroes in the movies?

In my view, Satan wants us to believe that us little ole' humans have nothing special about us and that any life outside of Earth has real power.  He wants us to believe that all intelligent life forms want to come to Earth to kill us and farm us and strip Earth of its' natural resources.  He wants us to believe that alien life is more intelligent than us because they have more impressive weaponry and they have discovered how to travel in time and come to Earth; while we have barely figured out how to get to the moon.

Why is this important to look at?  It's important because if Satan can get us to think any and all life forms that are not from Earth are suspect and are only interested in human life to farm us and kill us, maybe, just maybe we will subconsciously begin to believe that since God, Jesus and the Holy Spirit aren't from Earth that they fall into that harmful, anti-human category as well. Satan doesn't give a fuck if you believe demons and him fall into that human-hating category just so long as you believe that God, Jesus and the Holy Spirit are in there.

The other aspect of superheroes I don't like the media pushing is that you have to have special powers that are either man-made, come from a freak accident of science or were given to you by a peaceful, alien life-form somehow.  Why is that such a big deal?  With all the superhero movies pushing this theme, it makes is easier for us to subconsciously believe we don't have the power of God inside us from birth.  It makes us feel like we are powerless unless we are in a freak accident and can turn green and smash shit every time we get mad.  These movies program us

that having faith in God won't save us but faith in each other, faith

in the power of human ability and faith in the power of

superheroes is the only way to save the day.

Our view on superheros is important because we need to

stop believing the cartoon hype and start believing that each of us

has power and is superhuman because we have the supernatural

power of God inside us from birth and that power is unmatched!

That power can't be copied with any stories of superheroes no

matter how the media tries and pushes it on us.  What if…

# CLASH OF THE CULTURES:  CUSS/SLANG WORDS

In any relationship, communication seems to be the bonding agent.  Couples therapy involves seeking ways to communicate better.  Corporations constantly look for the best ways to communicate and reach their target audience.  Different cultures communicate within their culture one way and with other cultural groups another way.  To be effective in our personal, business and cross-cultural communications, I believe a better understanding of cuss and slang words needs to be discussed.

Purpose of cuss/slang words:

1.  In general, these words are words to convey a high level of emotion or passion.  It gives your mind a break from all the formality of our language and lets you enter a more creative frame of mind because some things can't always be put into words. Example:  You are driving down the highway and a car, not just any car, a new model Lamborghini races by doin' no less than 130mph.  If I'm telling you about it and I say "I was driving on the Lodge Freeway heading downtown and I was doing about 90mph;  when all of a sudden I hear this loud ass roaring sound and this bright red Lamborghini or some shit blows by like I'm fuckin' standin' still!  He had to be doing at least 160 fuckin miles an hour!  That shit was crazy!"  What should that tell you about my character if anything?  What was my excitement/passion level and how could

you tell?  What does my choice of words say about my education level?  What does my choice of words say about my spirituality?

- You can't really tell much about me as a person by my response.  You can't say I'm a bad dad or a good one; that I'm rich or poor.
- You can tell my excitement level was off the charts.
- You can't tell whether or not I graduated high school or if I have a Master's Degree in International Finance.
- You can't even tell if I'm a Christian or not.  If someone can show me in the Bible where it says "the use of a particular word to describe the indescribable is a sin"……

2. Cuss/slang words allow the user to give others warnings as to where they are at emotionally.  Example:  Somebody keeps calling your phone or sending you text and is annoying you.  I text back "Leave me the fuck alone!"  What should that tell you about my character if anything?  What was my excitement/passion level and how could you tell?  What does my choice of words say about my education level?  What does my choice of words say about my spirituality?

- You can't tell much about my character by my response.  You can't say I'm a good dad or a bad one; that I'm rich or poor.
- You can tell my emotions are running hot and on a high level.

- You can't tell my education level by my response.
- You can't even tell if I am a Christian or not. There is nowhere in the Bible that says you have to only use certain words to describe your mood when you're angry. It does say "don't do anything in anger" and I believe that refers to actual actions or regarding the use of language you shouldn't say something in anger that you will regret. To me, letting you know that I've had enough and giving you a verbal warning is fair.

3. Believe it or not, cuss/slang words can be a "term of endearment". What is better for a boss to say to a good employee: "Daryl, I think you are the best employee ever! You are always on time and never complain!! You work lots of overtime when needed and I value you on my team!" or "Hey Daryl, I just wanna let you know that you tha fuckin man around here." What should that tell you about my character if anything? What was my excitement/passion level and how could you tell? What does my choice of words say about my education level? What does my choice of words say about my spirituality?

   - You can't tell anything about my character. You can't say I'm a good dad or a bad one; that I'm rich or poor.
   - You can tell that my praise level for my employee is high and involves so many different aspects that I know I can say what I said and he would know what it is without me going into a drawn out list.

- You can't tell my level of education by my response.
- You can't tell if I am a Christian or not. Nowhere does it say that there are specific words you should use when giving someone praise or acknowledgement.

4. Special case words:  nigga, bitch.. In various parts of the world the word "black" is negro, negru or nero.  During the period of African American slavery in America, white people called black people Negroes and the slang term became "nigger".  Oddly enough, that term has become a widely accepted term of unification among black people. During slavery, the slave families were all separated and sold off to different plantations and it became impossible to say the name of the family who you were related to. The only name/term that all blacks had in common was "nigger".  Whether you were light or dark complexion, you were equally treated unequally under the law as a "nigger".  It has even become a term used by other cultures to mean "homeboy/close friend". Regarding the word "bitch".  I know females who use that term on the regular basis as though it's the female version of nigga.  At the same time, a man can call that same female a bitch and a fight will break out.  Men even use that term with each other and it could be considered a good or bad thing.  What should that tell you about my character if anything?  What was my excitement/passion level and how could you tell?  What does my choice of words say about my education level?  What does my choice of words say about my spirituality?

- You can't tell anything about my character. You can't tell whether I'm a good dad or a bad one; whether I'm rich or poor.
- You can tell my passion level only if you understand the pitch and tone when I use that word.
- You can't tell if I dropped out of school or have a Doctor's Degree in Brain Anatomy.
- You can tell nothing about my spirituality when I use that term

5. Business and cuss/slang words is very tricky because in business dealings you have to be aware of cultural differences regarding politics, word choice and a host of other factors to be able to communicate effectively. Example: I have a brother who has a professional service company. When him and I talk or when he talks to black clients, there is one "language" used; but when a white client comes in, a whole different "language" is used. Depending on who brings what to the table determines the language. I have been around important business meetings where the guy who thought he was in charge was able to cuss but no one else dared; and I have seen meetings where nobody cussed...until certain people walked out the room.

   - You can't tell how sharp a person is in business by whether or not he cusses or uses slang. Is a person who refrains from using cuss/slang words until after the meeting better than a person who uses it during a meeting?
   - You can't tell his pedigree either.

- You can't tell his spirituality either.

**Conclusion:**  The bottom line is that you can't properly judge a person by their use or lack of use, of these words.  You are not a better Christian by not using these words.  Your segment of a cultural group is no better than another segment of a different cultural group.

**Solutions**

- Read the situation before you speak.
- Understand that if you use cuss/slang words they may be a barrier to cross cultural communication.  At the same time, if you don't use them, that can also be a barrier to communication.  In those settings BOTH parties should try and understand the other one's use of the language.
  - Cuss/slang words convey emotions. Emotions can be cultural based and complicated.  Once you understand the emotional impact of words, tread softly...or not.

# Personal Development Notes

# Personal Development Notes

# Personal Development Notes

# Personal Development Notes

# Personal Development Notes

www.ingramcontent.com/pod-product-compliance
Lightning Source LLC
Chambersburg PA
CBHW070132260726
48658CB00001B/379